SIMPLY SCIENCE

Soil

by Alice K. Flanagan

Content Adviser: Terrence E. Young Jr., M.Ed., M.L.S.,
Jefferson Parish (La.) Public Schools

Reading Adviser: Dr. Linda D. Labbo,
Department of Reading Education, College of Education,
The University of Georgia

 COMPASS POINT BOOKS

Minneapolis, Minnesota

Compass Point Books
3722 West 50th Street, #115
Minneapolis, MN 55410

Visit Compass Point Books on the Internet at *www.compasspointbooks.com* or e-mail your request to *custserv@compasspointbooks.com*

Photographs ©:
Jim Linna/FPG International, cover; Marilyn Moseley LaMantia, 4; Robert McCaw, 5; Index Stock Imagery, 6; Robert McCaw, 7; VCG/FPG International, 8; International Stock/John Guider Photography, 9; Marilyn Moseley LaMantia, 10; International Stock/ Tom Grimm, 11; Root Resources/Bill Glass, 12; Unicorn Stock Photos/Wayne Floyd, 13; Index Stock Imagery, 15; Photo Network, Bill Bachmann, 16; Visuals Unlimited, Mark E. Gibson, 17; Marilyn Moseley LaMantia, 18; Visuals Unlimited/Joe McDonald, 19; Index Stock Imagery, 20, 21, 22; James P. Rowan, 23; Root Resources/Louise K. Broman, 24; International Stock/Wood Sabold, 25; Unicorn Stock Photos/Aneal Vohra, 26; Index Stock Imagery, 27; Marilyn Moseley LaMantia, 28.

Editors: E. Russell Primm and Emily J. Dolbear
Photo Researcher: Svetlana Zhurkina
Photo Selector: Dawn Friedman
Design: Bradfordesign, Inc.

Library of Congress Cataloging-in-Publication Data

Flanagan, Alice K.
    Soil / by Alice K. Flanagan.
        p. cm. — (Simply science)
    Includes bibliographical references (p.   ) and index.
    Summary: Briefly describes the composition of different types of soil, the variety of plants and animals that live in it, and the necessity of soil to human life.
    ISBN 0-7565-0035-4 (hardcover : lib. bdg.)
        1. Soil ecology—Juvenile literature. 2. Soils—Juvenile literature. [1. Soil ecology. 2. Ecology. 3. Soils.] I. Title. II. Simply science (Minneapolis, Minn.)
    QH541.5.S6 F63 2000
    577.5'7—dc21   00-008559

Table of Contents

Looking at Soil

Soil covers most of the land on Earth. It is also one of the most important things on Earth. Without soil, we could not live. And it's right outside your door. Pick up some soil from your backyard or from a potted plant. Hold it in your hand. What color is it? Does it have a smell? Look at the soil through a magnifying glass. What do you see?

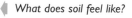

What does soil feel like?

Water and wind can wear down rocks to make soil.

Weathering Rock

Soil is made partly of little bits of rock. Weather breaks up rock into these tiny pieces. Wind, water, heat, and ice wear away the rock. This is called weathering, or **erosion**.

As streams flow downhill from mountains, they carry rocks with them. When waves crash against rocks, the rocks break apart. Wind, rain, heat, and cold can crack rocks. Sometimes young trees grow in the cracks. As the trees grow, they force the rocks apart.

A waterfall wears down a mountain and carries away rocks.

Water eroded this farmland.

Very tiny pieces of rock are called sand. Even smaller pieces turn into clay. If you look closely, you can see rock being weathered at the beach or in the park, or even in your backyard.

What Is Soil Made Of?

Soil is made up of more than bits of rock, of course. Leaves and twigs fall from trees onto the soil. Animals leave their droppings on the soil. And all living things become part of soil when they die.

The sand at this beach is made of tiny pieces of rock.

Dead leaves become part of soil ▶ on the forest floor.

Most soil contains billions of tiny living things. They are so tiny that you cannot see them. These living things are called **bacteria**, **molds**, and one-celled animals. They feed on dead plants and animals that fall to the ground. They make the dead plants and animals rot, or decay.

The part of the soil that contains rotting plants and animals is called **humus**. Humus feeds plants that grow in the soil. It also helps the soil to hold water.

◀ *Humus is dark and moist.*

Seedlings grow into big trees in the forest. ▶

Plants and Animals

Plants help the soil too. They cover it and keep it from being carried away by wind and rain. Plant roots grow down into the soil and help hold it together.

Animals are also important to soil. Earthworms, ants, and beetles make spaces when they crawl through the soil. Then fresh air can reach plants and animals underground, and water can get to the plant roots.

◀ Ants and early insect forms called larvae in the soil

An earthworm crawls through soil. ▶

Water, air, warmth, and light bring life to soil. Without them, plants and animals would not grow in the soil. And without plants and animals in the soil, larger animals would have nothing to eat. Plants and animals make the soil rich in food.

The new leaves of a young plant ▶

Topsoil

Soil covers most of the land on Earth. The only places without soil are mountains and places so cold that they have always been covered in ice. The first few inches of soil are called **topsoil**. This is the best part of the soil. Good topsoil has lots of food for plants and tiny animals. Things grow best in good topsoil.

Antarctica has no soil because it is all ice.

The rocky top of a mountain has no soil.

Topsoil takes hundreds of years to form. There are three kinds of topsoil— forest soil, grassland soil, and desert soil. Each type of soil is formed in a different kind of weather—hot or cold and wet or dry. And each type of soil has different kinds of plants and animals. The United States and Canada have all three kinds of soil.

You can buy topsoil in a bag for your garden.

Chola cactus thrives in New Mexico.

Forest Soils

Forest soils are warm, damp, and rich in humus. In these forests, the weather is hot. They get a lot of rain. Trees grow well in forest soil. Billions of tiny plants and animals live there too.

The moist forest floor is perfect for these ferns.

Many different kinds of trees can grow in a forest.

Grassland Soils

Grassland soils are formed in warm areas where there is some rainfall. Summers are hot and dry. Winters are wet and cold. Trees cannot live in this kind of weather, but grass grows well. With good rainfall, food crops grow well there, too. Grassland soil is dark and rich.

Grasslands are good for growing crops and feeding cows.

Grasses growing on a prairie ▶

Desert Soil

Desert soil is partly sand. It has little humus in it. You might think that nothing could grow in desert soil. It is true that few plants grow in the hot, dry desert. But if there is a sudden rainfall, flowers bloom and fruit grows. Desert soil can be **fertile—** it can produce living things.

 Sandy desert soil

A cactus can grow in the desert ▶
with very little water.

Caring for the Land

Animals eat the grasses and grains grown in soil. We eat the plants and animals. If we dump chemicals and waste in the soil, animals and plants will die. Farmers will not be able to grow their crops in the soil. The soil of Earth is a precious gift. We must take care of it.

◀ Freshly seeded cropland

We must take care of the soil so we all have healthy food to eat. ▶

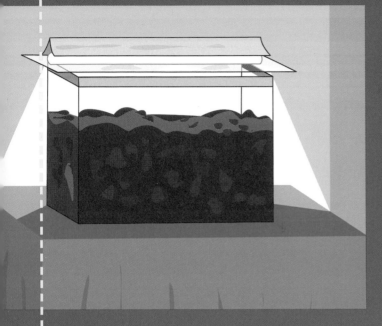

Fill a large aquarium with soil, dead grass, and leaves.

In time, plants will grow in the soil.

Learn for Yourself

One sunny winter day, dig up some soil from your backyard or nearby park. Be sure to ask an adult first! You'll need soil that has dead grass and leaves in it. Put the soil in a large glass jar or an **aquarium**. Water the soil well. Put netting over the top. Then partly cover it with a piece of plastic wrap and put it near a light.

As the soil gets warm, insects that were resting, or **hibernating**, in the soil will start to move about. Soon, you will see plants sending up green shoots. Things come to life when there is warmth, air, water, and light.

Glossary

aquarium—a glass tank where water animals and plants are kept

bacteria—tiny living things

erosion—wearing away by wind, water, heat, and ice

fertile—able to produce plants and crops

hibernating—resting or sleeping for the winter

humus—rotting vegetables and plants

mold—a woolly substance that grows on old food and other things

topsoil—the top few inches of soil, rich with food for plants and animals

Did You Know?

- Soil scientists are called pedologists.

- Soil colors range from yellow and red to dark brown and black.

- There are more than 70,000 kinds of soil in the United States.

- About 5 to 10 tons of animal life can live in 1 acre (0.4 hectare) of soil.

Want to Know More?

At the Library

Bryant-Mole, Karen. *Soil.* Austin, Tex.: Raintree Steck-Vaughn, 1996.

Fowler, Allan. *Animals under the Ground.* Danbury, Conn.: Children's Press, 1997.

On the Web

Athena: Earth and Space Science for K–12

http://www.athena.ivv.nasa.gov/index.html

For information about many science subjects, including instructional material

kinderGARDEN

http://aggie-horticulture.tamu.edu/kindergarden/kinder.htm

For an introduction to the many ways children can interact with plants and the outdoors

What on Earth Is Soil?

http://pelican.gmpo.gov/edresources/soil.html

For a list of quick facts about soil and its uses

Through the Mail

Soil and Water Conservation Society

7515 NE Ankeny Road

Ankeny, IA 50021

For information about soil and water management and the environment

On the Road

Brooklyn Botanic Garden

1000 Washington Avenue

Brooklyn, NY 11225

718/623-7200

Botanic gardens are wonderful places to visit. This one has more than 12,000 kinds of plants from around the world.

Index

About the Author

Alice K. Flanagan writes books for children and teachers. Ever since she was a young girl, she has enjoyed writing. She has written more than seventy books on a wide variety of topics. Some of her books include biographies of U.S. presidents and their wives, biographies of people working in our neighborhoods, phonics books for beginning readers, and informational books about birds and Native Americans. Alice K. Flanagan lives in Chicago, Illinois.